BoHo Designs

Coloring Book #5

W9-AXP-426

18 Fun Designs + See How Colors Play Together + Creative Ideas

MEET THE ARTIST:
Valori Wells

Photo by Valori Wells

Valori is an artist, fabric designer, quiltmaker, photographer, author, and owner of a quilt store with her mother. She lives in beautiful Sisters, Oregon. Valori loves taking photos and is inspired by everything she sees around her.

She designs fabrics that quiltmakers and other sewists love to use. Her fabrics include larger-than-life images inspired by nature in fresh colors.

The patterns in this coloring book are some of Valori's original fabric designs. Her designs are so fun. They are full of flowers, birds, and even elephants. They give your imagination a lot of room to play. Be Boho and use whatever colors you like in them. (Boho is short for *Bohemian*, a fashion style that is free-spirited, arty, and unconventional.)

Photo by C&T Publishing

Photo by Valori Wells

Photo by Valori Wells

"My hope is to inspire you to make a wish and fly—to create from your heart."

Do You Know How Fabric Is Designed?

All the fabric that you see around you—from your clothes to your bedspread—is designed by fabric designers. Fabric designers are artists, and fabric is like big blank pieces of paper to them. Depending on how the fabric will be used, they decide what it will look like. It might have a lot of bright colors and geometric shapes such as circles and triangles. Or it might have colors from nature and feature flowers.

Artists (including fabric designers) often use color wheels to find good color combinations to use. Be sure to look inside the back cover for a color wheel that you can use to see how colors play together.

Valori's designs are sold by Robert Kaufman Fabrics.

FunStitch STUDIO

Hashley

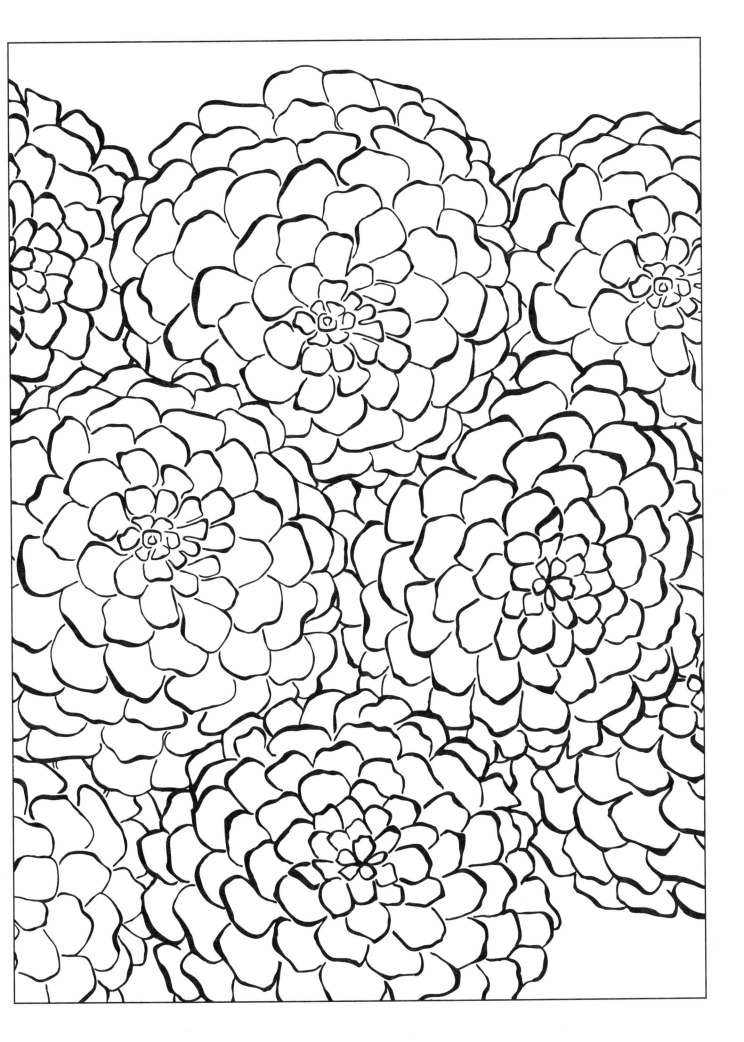

Quilt Note

Imagine the fun you'll have transforming a simple sweatshirt into a designer original. In this book you will learn how to add zippers, plackets, drawstring hems, cuffs, binding, pockets, elbow patches and much more to make an ordinary sweatshirt into something truly unique. Whether you need a dressy cardigan or a sporty pullover, you can create it from a sweatshirt with the tips and techniques provided. We've even included some fun designs for kids.

Table of Contents

General Instructions

BEFORE YOU BEGIN

Sweatshirt Selection
Choose a good-quality sweatshirt of 100 percent cotton or cotton/polyester-blend fleece. Avoid 100 percent acrylic fleece; it will pill under the arms and anywhere else there is wear—even normal wear. Selecting a dense fleece is especially important when planning an appliquéd design. A dense fabric will resist rippling during machine-appliqué steps.

Prewashing
Prewash and dry the sweatshirt and all fabrics, using no fabric softener. Fabric softeners can interfere with the gripping power of fusible web products. Press with a steam iron to remove any excess wrinkles.

When the sweatshirt and fabric are not washed before construction, expect a disaster after the first washing. The fabrics will probably not shrink at the same rate, causing unsightly puckering, and all your work will be for nothing.

Pressing
After binding, press the entire sweatshirt with a steam iron set on a medium setting. This really gives the garment a finished look. Many sewing and quilting teachers try to impress on their students that much of the styling of a garment occurs with the iron and not the sewing machine.

Supplies & Tools
Some basic supplies and tools include a sewing machine, usual sewing supplies, pencil, scissors, iron, ironing board, self-healing mat, rotary cutter, ruler and chalk pencil or fade-out pen.

CHOOSING A SWEATSHIRT STYLE

Sweatshirt Styles
Sweatshirts are available in almost any color and in a variety of styles. Choose the style to best enhance your chosen design. For example, a raglan-sleeve sweatshirt would not work if you plan to outline the armhole seam with patchwork. For this type of stitching, the armhole seam is necessary.

Classic Pullover. Always a favorite for comfort and casual wearability, the classic pullover sweatshirt offers a blank canvas for a variety of piecing and appliqué techniques. The sleeves can either be set in or raglan. Some designs require the use of a set-in sleeve to be successful.

Cropped Pullover. This sweatshirt has the same comfy style as the classic pullover, but is shorter, usually skimming the waistline. A drawstring in a casing is a nice way to add interest to a cropped pullover.

Bolero. This style usually has no closure or the closure is a simple frog. It makes a dressy jacket and can be worn in almost any length.

Cardigan. A good way to finish a cardigan front is with a placket. It stabilizes the front to support buttons, snaps or other closures.

Bomber Jacket. Styled similarly to a baseball jacket, this can be a shortened version or as long as the original sweatshirt.

Vest. The properties of sweatshirt fleece make it easy to remove sleeves completely for a vest effect. Just remember to stabilize the armholes to prevent stretching out of shape.

NECKLINE VARIATIONS

Finding the Sweatshirt Center

1. Fold the sweatshirt in half, matching shoulder seams, sleeves and hem ribbing as shown in Figure 1.

Figure 1

2. Mark along the fold with a chalk pencil or fade-out pen.

Ribbing

There is absolutely nothing wrong with leaving the ribbing on any style sweatshirt. If you choose to open the front, such as for making a cardigan or bomber jacket style, it's nice to finish the ribbing for a professional look. Fold the neck-edge ribbing under as shown in Figure 2; stitch in place by hand or machine as shown in Figure 3.

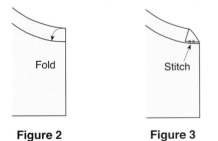

Fold

Stitch

Figure 2   **Figure 3**

Binding With Bias Binding

Another popular type of neckline finish is to carefully cut the ribbing from the neckline with sharp scissors. Try to cut as close to the ribbing stitching as possible to enlarge the neckline as little as possible. Then bind with commercial, double-fold bias binding or self-made binding using fabrics to match sweatshirt referring to one of the preparation methods on page 10.

SLEEVE FINISHES

Cuffs

Cuffs are a fun way to change the look of a sweatshirt. To add the look of a cuff without the bulk of the folded fabric, refer to the following instructions.

1. Cut the ribbing off the bottom edge of each sleeve.

2. Try the sweatshirt on to determine the desired length of the sleeve. The sleeve will fit differently without the bulk of ribbing. Cut sleeves to be the same length.

3. Cut two pieces of fabric 6" by the circumference of the sleeve plus 1".

4. Fold each cuff piece in half with short ends aligned and right sides together to make a tube as shown in Figure 4. Stitch along short edges using a ½" seam allowance; press seam open. Repeat with remaining cuff piece.

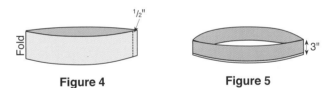

Figure 4   **Figure 5**

5. Fold each cuff tube in half along length with wrong sides together to make 3"-wide, double-layer tubes referring to Figure 5; press.

6. Pin a cuff tube to the right side raw edge of each sleeve as shown in Figure 6; stitch to sleeves using a ⅜" seam allowance.

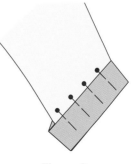

Figure 6

HEMLINE FINISHES

Ribbing

Ribbing is a great way to finish a pullover, cropped pullover or bomber jacket–style sweatshirt. If the sweatshirt is to be embellished only with an appliqué motif, there is probably no reason to do anything to the ribbing. If, however, the appliqué needs to be at the bottom edge of the sweatshirt, or for some other reason the bottom edge needs to be straight rather than gathered during embellishment, cut the ribbing off. It can always be reattached after embellishment is complete.

When to remove hemline ribbing
- When using a panel design.
- When working with a border design.
- When finishing with binding or casing.
- When shortening a sweatshirt.
- When creating a bolero-style sweatshirt.
- When placing an appliqué close to the hemline.
- When an elbow patch requires many turns in a narrow space and the sweatshirt needs to be opened along the underarm seam.

Drawstring

It is easy to add a casing of a coordinating or contrasting fabric to accommodate a drawstring at the hemline.

1. Determine distance around hemline; add 1". Prepare a 3"-wide bias casing strip the determined length for a wide casing or a 2"-wide strip for a narrow casing referring to page 10 for preparing bias yardage, steps 1–5.

2. Fold the strip in half along length with wrong sides together to make a double layer; press to make a crease.

3. Unfold the strip and find the center point; bond a small piece of fusible interfacing in place above the crease as shown in Figure 7.

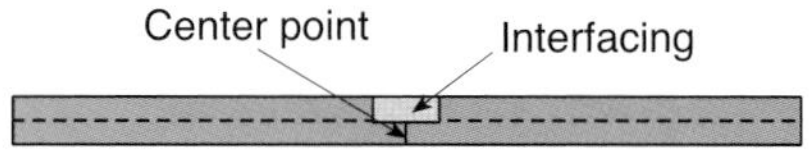

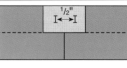

Figure 7

4. Work two buttonholes ½" apart in stabilized casing section as shown in Figure 8.

Figure 8

5. Fold casing strip matching short ends with right sides together; stitch a ½" seam allowance. Press seam open.

6. Refold casing strip along creased line with wrong sides together; pin.

7. Insert drawstring in casing; pull ends through buttonholes.

8. Pin casing strip center at center front of sweatshirt with raw edges even. Stitch in place using a ½" seam allowance.

9. Fold seam allowances to inside of sweatshirt; topstitch ⅛" above casing through all layers to hold seam allowance in place.

Finishing With Bias Binding

1. Measure the distance around the bottom edge of the sweatshirt; add 1" to this measurement.

2. Create bias binding yardage from one or more fabrics referring to pages 10–11.

3. Refer to pages 11–12 for hints on applying binding to the sweatshirt hemline.

FRONT FINISHES

Placket

A fabric placket offers the security of a stable front overlap without changing the size of the sweatshirt. It is a good finish for a cardigan.

1. Cut two 4"-wide by length of jacket strips from fabric and two 3"-wide matching length strips of fusible interfacing 1" shorter than fabric strips.

2. Center interfacing on the wrong side of each fabric strip; fuse in place referring to manufacturer's instructions.

3. Fold each strip in half along length with wrong sides together; press.

4. Unfold, and then fold each strip in half with right sides together. Stitch across one short end through both layers using a ½" seam allowance. Clip corner; trim seam allowance to ¼" as shown in Figure 9. Repeat with remaining strip.

Trim to ¹/₄"

Clip corner

Figure 9

5. Open fold; position one strip along the cut center on the jacket with right sides together with seam at the top of the neckline. Stitch in place with a ½" seam allowance; press seam allowances and placket toward the center line.

6. Fold the placket strip to the wrong side; turn under ½" along remaining long raw edge. Stitch in place along wrong side of jacket by hand or machine. Repeat on remaining center-front edge.

7. Work evenly spaced buttonholes in the right-front placket to fit chosen buttons.

8. Stitch buttons in place on left-front placket to match buttonholes.

Zipper Front

A jacket zipper with big nylon teeth adds a professional touch to a customized sweat-shirt. Cut the sweatshirt to the desired length before purchasing the zipper.

1. Find center and cut sweatshirt front apart.

2. Prepare 1½ yards 2"-wide bias binding referring to page 10.

3. Fold ½" to the wrong side along one long edge.

4. Bind both center-front edges of the sweatshirt referring to pages 11–12, finishing the top and bottom of each front binding piece.

5. Position the zipper behind the binding and topstitch zipper tape in place along edge of binding.

EMBELLISHMENTS

Appliqué

Appliqué is a very popular method of embellishing fabric surfaces of all kinds, including sweatshirts.

1. Place tracing paper on pattern; trace with pencil. Cut out shapes on traced lines.

2. Trace shapes onto the paper side of fusible web following manufacturer's instructions and as directed on the patterns for number to cut. *Note: If many shapes are to be cut from the same fabric, bond the fusible web to the wrong side of the fabric and trace shapes onto the paper side of the fused fabric. Cut out shapes, leaving a margin around each one.*

3. Fuse shapes to the wrong side of the fabrics referring to pattern for color. Cut out shapes on traced lines; remove paper backing.

4. Place fabric cutout in the desired position on the sweatshirt and fuse in place.

5. Cut a piece of fabric stabilizer larger than fused shapes and secure to the wrong side of the sweatshirt under fused shapes.

6. Stitch around each fused shape with either matching or contrasting thread, using a machine satin stitch and beginning with back-most pieces first.

7. When stitching is complete, remove fabric stabilizer.

8. Press appliqués with a steam iron for a smooth finish.

Elbow Patches

1. If applying a block or appliqué piece on the sleeves for elbow patches, try the sweatshirt on to determine position of the patch.

2. Pin in place, then remove the sweatshirt.

3. Check position of patches; they should be in the same position on each sleeve.

4. Before bonding the patches in place, test the pinned patch on the sewing machine. Is the sleeve large enough to accommodate the turns necessary to stitch this patch in place?

5. If sleeve is not large enough, consider opening the sweatshirt along the side/underarm seam, stitching the patch in place and then closing the seam with a serger or overcast zigzag stitch.

6. Once you have assured the feasibility of stitching the patch in place, bond it in position using fusible web.

7. Stabilize, stitch, remove stabilizer and press as for appliqué.

Passementerie or Decorative Trims

Add movement and a range of looks with narrow fusible bias binding or couched ribbon, cord, etc.

1. Mark desired lines on the sweatshirt with chalk pencil or fade-out pen.

Tips for Smooth Appliqué
- Use a stabilizer on the wrong side of the sweatshirt to prevent ripples. An iron-on, peel-off stabilizer is helpful to prevent stretching.
- When stitching is complete, remove stabilizer before wearing.
- Tweezers will help remove small bits of stabilizer between too-close rows of satin stitches.
- Use a narrow satin stitch for small appliqué pieces or those with many turns. Use a medium-width satin stitch for larger pieces.
- Work satin stitches with rayon thread to coordinate or contrast with the appliqué shape in the top of the machine and matching all-purpose thread in the bobbin.
- Use a new needle or needle with a good point. Any burr from a pin or a blunt point from repeated usage will cause skipped stitches.
- Loosen the tension on the top thread slightly to allow the bobbin thread to pull the top thread to the wrong side of the sweatshirt.

2. Stabilize on the wrong side with iron-on, peel-off stabilizer.

3. For fusible bias binding, lay the binding on the marked line; fuse in place using an iron wand or craft iron, turning beginning and stopping ends under 1/8".

4. Straight-stitch close to each edge of binding and across end using all-purpose or metallic thread to match binding in the top of the machine and matching all-purpose thread in the bobbin.

5. For couched ribbon or cord, lay ribbon/cord on the marked line; hold in place with temporary fabric adhesive.

6. Stitch in place using a wide zigzag stitch worked over the ribbon/cord as shown in Figure 10 using coordinated thread or clear nylon monofilament in the top of the machine and all-purpose thread in the bobbin.

Figure 10

Hints for Applying Decorative Trims

- Mark design lines with chalk pencil or fade-out pen.
- Add a stabilizer to the wrong side of the fabric under the area to be stitched.
- Use a tiny craft iron or wand to make the fusing step progress quickly.
- Use a pair of tweezers to help pick stabilizer from between close rows of stitches.
- Choose a dense fleece to resist puckers and ripples while turning sweatshirt during stitching steps.

Prairie Pockets

A closed fabric pocket adds dimension and interest to a sweatshirt. It's a welcome relief from the math necessary for square-in-a-square block designs.

1. Cut two squares of fabric (practice with 4" x 4" squares). Cut a slit in one square as shown in Figure 11.

Figure 11

2. Place the squares right sides together; stitch around all sides.

3. Trim corners; turn right side out through the slit cut in one of the squares. Hand-stitch the opening closed with an overcast stitch; press.

4. Position the square on a background square as shown in Figure 12; place a pin in the center of each side. Hand-tack in place at each pin.

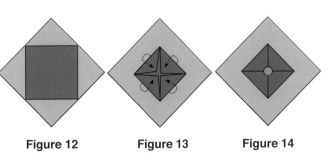

Figure 12 **Figure 13** **Figure 14**

5. Fold points to the center as shown in Figure 13, and anchor with a button referring to Figure 14 or a decorative knot worked in pearl cotton or 4 strands of embroidery floss.

Tips for Adding Dimension

- Substitute prairie points for triangles in a block or prairie pockets for squares.
- Use layers of appliqué fabric with raw edges to create a fringed effect when the sweatshirt is laundered.
- Highlight appliqué motifs with ribbon embroidery or floss embroidery.
- Use caution when placing dimensional items such as buttons, beads or charms, to avoid direct contact with skin or creating an uncomfortable lump when sitting in a chair.

BLOCK DESIGNS

Individual Blocks

A sweatshirt is a dandy place to use sampler blocks you've never assembled into a bed-size quilt. For variety, consider using a block design with no background pieces. Such a design can be used in many different settings as shown in Figure 15. Notice we have avoided unattractive placement in the bust-line area. Also, the turns required to use this block design as an elbow would have required that the sweatshirt be opened along the side/underarm seams.

Figure 15

Panel Style

Blocks may be stitched together to create panels for a cardigan as shown in Figure 16. These panels should never stabilize the neckline or interfere with its ability to stretch, unless an opening, such as a front placket, is provided. Remember that the neck ribbing on the sweatshirt is meant to stretch to fit over your head. Any patchwork addition should not interfere with this or you will find yourself with a neckline that won't stretch to enable it to be slipped over the head!

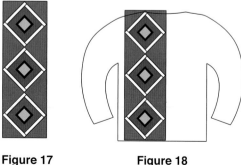

Figure 16

Tips for Motif Placement

- Avoid placing single motifs in the bust area.
- Place any block design on the back above or below dead center to avoid the bull's-eye effect.
- Consider multiple sizes of the motif for variety and interest when using more than one block of the same design.
- Want to add elbow patches? Keep the motif simple, such as a square, rectangle, oval or round shape for easy maneuvering in sleeves when stitching.

Cardigans With Panels

1. Stitch blocks together to create a panel as shown in Figure 17; press. The panel should be equal to the length of the sweatshirt front as shown in Figure 18.

Figure 17   **Figure 18**

2. Cut border strips at least 2" wide, joining along short ends, if necessary, to create strips as long as the panel edges.

3. Stitch one strip to each long side of the panel to create a pieced unit. Press under raw edges of outer strip ¼" on each panel as shown in Figure 19.

1/4"

Figure 19

4. Position one panel on each side of the center-front line of sweatshirt, folded seam allowance toward side seam of sweatshirt and raw bottom edges of the pieced panel even with raw cut edges of the sweatshirt hemline; pin in place.

5. Mark the shoulder line of the sweatshirt on the pieced panel ½" larger than the sweatshirt as shown in Figure 20.

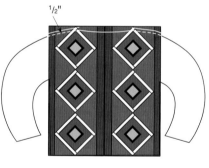

1/2"

Figure 20

6. Mark the neckline of the sweatshirt on the pieced panel, again referring to Figure 20; trim the panel even with the neckline.

7. Turn ½" to wrong side of top shoulder edge of panel, making folded edges even with sweatshirt shoulder line. Stitch across the shoulder line with a straight stitch or narrow zigzag stitch, using thread to match fabrics or clear nylon monofilament in the top of the machine and all-purpose thread to match sweatshirt in the bobbin. Pivot at the neckline and baste through all layers. Pivot at center-front line and baste through all layers. Pivot at hemline and baste through all layers. Stitch along outer edge through sweatshirt and fold of pieced panel.

8. Cut sweatshirt along center-front line.

9. Bind neckline, center-front and bottom edge referring to binding instructions on pages 11–12 to finish.

10. Press finished sweatshirt with steam iron.

Pullover With Covered Front

1. Remove hemline ribbing.

2. Mark center-front line of sweatshirt with chalk pencil.

3. Prepare a pieced panel using leftover strip-pieced sections or a prepared pieced panel at least 1" larger than sweatshirt width and length. Mark panel centers.

4. Position pieced panel on sweatshirt, matching center lines on panel with center line on sweatshirt with top edge of panel ½" above shoulder seam as shown in Figure 21.

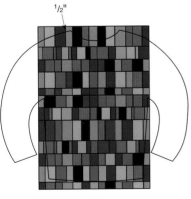

Figure 21

5. Mark neckline and shoulder line and sides on each side of panel with chalk pencil, again referring to Figure 21. Mark ½" away from first line for seam allowance; cut panel along outer marked line.

6. Press seam allowance to wrong side around all edges.

7. Pin pressed panel to sweatshirt, matching side seams, shoulder seams and center-front lines. Stitch along folded edges as in step 7 for Cardigan With Panels.

8. Press sweatshirt front; trim panel even with sweatshirt along bottom edge. Stitch along hemline through pieced panel and sweatshirt front.

9. Finish hem edge using desired method.

10. Press finished sweatshirt with steam iron.

Border Style

Blocks may be joined to create a wide band around the hemline of the sweatshirt. Since this would stabilize the hemline and limit its ability to stretch, the center front may be opened and the sweatshirt turned into a jacket or cardigan.

1. Find the center-front line of the sweatshirt as instructed on page 3. Mark with chalk pencil; cut open along marked center-front line.

2. Remove the ribbing along the hemline.

3. Stitch blocks together in a band long enough to reach around the sweatshirt at the hemline.

4. Cut border strips in a desired width to fit along long edges of blocks as shown in Figure 22. Stitch borders along the top and bottom of the block strip to prevent block design from being lost in the ribbing gathers later. Press ⅜" to the wrong side of one long edge of the pieced strip.

Figure 22

5. Position the pieced strip around the outside edges of the sweatshirt with short raw ends meeting at the center-front line and the long raw edges even with the cut edge of the sweatshirt hemline; pin in place.

6. Stitch along fold of band with a narrow zigzag or blind-hem stitch; baste through raw edges at bottom to hold together.

7. Stitch ribbing back onto sweatshirt at bottom edge or bind bottom edge referring to Hemline Finishes on page 4.

ADDING A HIDDEN POCKET

For fun, tuck hidden pockets inside large blocks or panels on a sweatshirt.

1. Cut four pocket pieces, (template on page 13) (reverse two) using coordinating fabrics.

2. Place two pocket pieces right sides together; stitch around outer edge with a ½" seam allowance as shown in Figure 23, leaving end open as indicated on pattern. Repeat with remaining pocket pieces; press a ¼" seam allowance to the wrong side along one open end as shown in Figure 24.

| Figure 23 | Figure 24 |

3. Place front panels or blocks right side up on work surface. Open pressed edge of border strip. Pin one pocket on outer edge of each panel 4"–6" from bottom with raw edges even and pressed seam allowance against panel as shown in Figure 25.

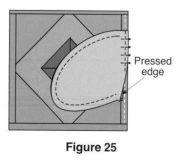

Pressed edge

Figure 25

4. Stitch through panel and top layer only of the pocket with a ¼" seam allowance. Fold to wrong side of panel; press.

5. Position one panel/pocket unit on each side of the center-front line of sweatshirt as shown in Figure 26, with folded seam allowance and pocket edge to the sweatshirt side, and raw bottom edge of the pieced panel even with the raw cut edge of the sweatshirt hemline.

Figure 26

6. Stitch along outer side edge through sweatshirt and fold of pieced panel border to the pocket opening as shown in Figure 27. Hold the pocket front open and stitch through the pocket back as shown in Figure 28. Stitch along remaining length of pieced panel side.

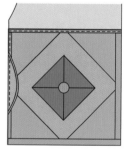

| Figure 27 | Figure 28 |

SECRETS TO PERFECT BINDING

Preparing Continuous Bias Binding

1. Cut one or two 18" x 18" squares of binding fabric. Cut each square on one diagonal to create two triangles as shown in Figure 29.

Figure 29

2. With right sides together, sew the two triangles together as shown in Figure 30; press seam open.

Figure 30

3. Mark lines every 2½" on the wrong side of the stitched unit as shown in Figure 31.

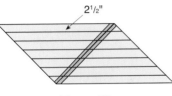

Figure 31

4. Bring the short ends together, right sides facing, offsetting one line as shown in Figure 32; stitch. The piece will now be a tube; press seam open. **Note**: *The stitched unit will look awkward.*

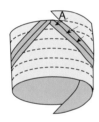

Figure 32

5. Begin cutting at point A and follow marked lines in a spiral fashion until all bias is cut in one continuous strip as shown in Figure 33.

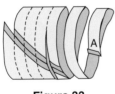

Figure 33

6. Fold binding strip in half along length with wrong sides together; press.

Binding Small Lengths

It is not necessary to construct continuous bias binding when you are finishing short lengths such as a single sleeve. Shorter strips work better for this type of binding.

1. Cut the specified-width strips along the bias of a width of fabric as shown in Figure 34; join the strips on the short ends to create longer yardage of bias as shown in Figure 35. Press seam allowances open to control bulk.

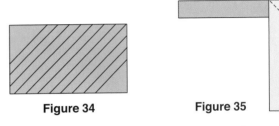

Figure 34   **Figure 35**

2. Fold long strip in half along length with wrong sides together; press.

Multi-Fabric Binding

Continuous bias binding may be made using more than one fabric. When binding a long length and using the continuous bias binding method, cut an 18" square of two different fabrics in half on the diagonal. Place triangles of different fabrics together as in step 2 for Preparing Continuous Bias Binding. Continue the procedure and you will create an interesting binding of alternating fabrics.

When binding a shorter length and using the small-length method, simply cut bias strips of the same width for different fabrics. Join along short ends and press seam allowances open to control bulk.

Applying Binding

1. Cut ribbing from edge to be bound.

2. Try on the sweatshirt to determine the desired length. Cut sleeves to the same length, unless the person has arms of two different lengths—this is fairly common.

3. Fold binding strip in half along length with wrong sides together; press to make a crease.

4. Position raw edges of binding right sides together along raw edge of sweatshirt sleeve, neck or hemline; stitch using a ⅜" seam allowance as shown in Figure 36.

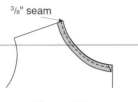

Figure 36

5. Fold stitched binding to the sweatshirt inside, encasing raw edges. Stitch in place by hand or machine using all-purpose thread to match fabrics or clear nylon monofilament in the top of the machine and all-purpose thread in the bobbin.

6. As an alternate method, leave the folded bias as a wider finished edge and finish the seam using a serger, or zigzag seam edges using a machine overcast stitch.

Beginning & Ending Binding
1. Begin stitching binding about 1" from the beginning end as shown in Figure 37.

Figure 37

2. Stitch to within approximately 2" from the end as shown in Figure 38.

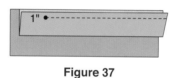

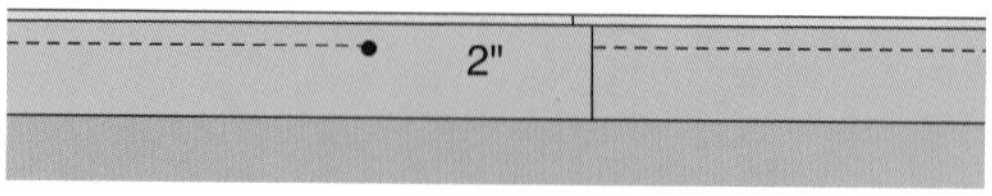

Figure 38

3. Open the binding and align ends of pieces with right sides together as shown in Figure 39. Stitch with a ¼" seam allowance; finger-press open to reduce bulk.

Figure 39

4. Trim excess binding; fold binding and complete stitching as shown in Figure 40.

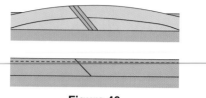

Figure 40

Turning Corners With Binding
1. Stitch to within ¼" of the corner as shown in Figure 41 (if you are using a ¼" seam allowance or whatever measurement equals the seam allowance); stop with the needle down in the sweatshirt. Lift pressure bar lever, leaving needle down and pivot the sweatshirt and binding. The excess binding will be turned into a mock miter later.

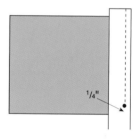

Figure 41

2. Resume stitching.

3. When folding binding to the other side of the sweatshirt, tuck the excess into a little pleat in the binding and hand-stitch closed as shown in Figure 42.

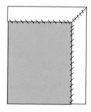

Figure 42

Binding Tips

- Steam curved edges by holding a steam iron slightly above the surface of the fabric. This helps smooth any puckered curves.
- Pull the binding slightly as you are stitching an inside curve. This changes the 1:1 ratio of binding to fabric and results in smooth inner curves. This only works for inside curves; this method can cause cupping of an outside curve.
- Start and stop binding in an unobtrusive spot, such as under an arm or at the side of a neckline.
- Don't press a neckline with the ribbing removed; it will stretch the neckline. Wait until the neckline has been stabilized with binding, or press before removing the binding.

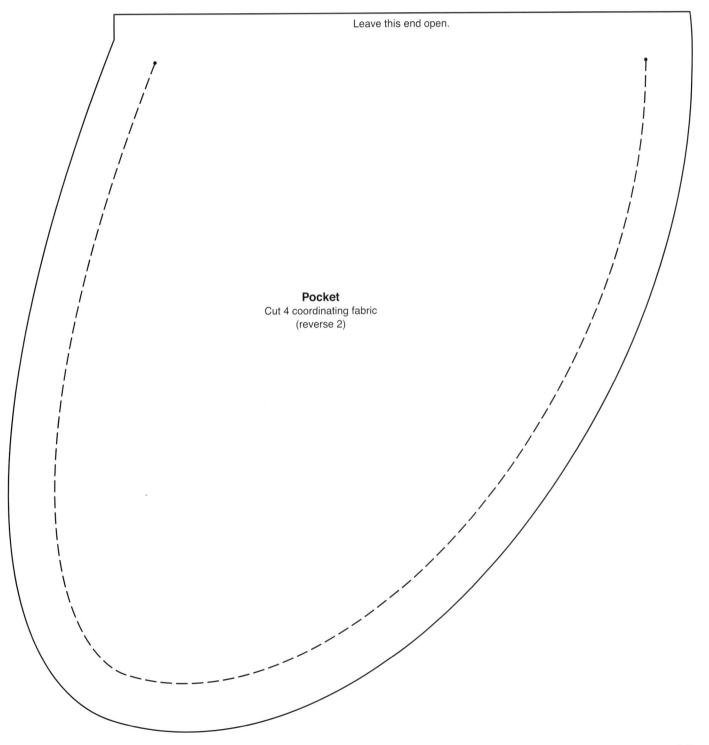

Leave this end open.

Pocket
Cut 4 coordinating fabric
(reverse 2)

Heavenly Hash

BY BETH WHEELER

Crazy-patch blocks in neutral hues of whites, creams and tans combine with gold embroidery in this stunning cardigan.

FABRIC
- 1 yard white-on-cream check for piecing and binding
- ¼ yard each 6–8 white-to-cream print fabrics

TOOLS & SUPPLIES
- Cream sweatshirt
- Off-white all-purpose thread
- Gold metallic thread
- Clear nylon monofilament
- ¼ yard lightweight interfacing
- Template material
- 5 (1") gold buttons
- Basic sewing tools and supplies and tracing paper

INSTRUCTIONS

1. Cut 20 squares lightweight interfacing 4½" x 4½".

2. Prepare templates for center shape using patterns given.

3. Cut center shapes from any fabric, varying number to cut from each shape to make 20 centers. Cut strips from remaining fabrics referring to Figure 1.

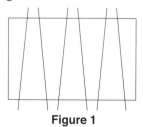

Figure 1

4. Position a center shape somewhere close to the center of an interfacing block; pin in place.

Lay a strip along any edge of the center shape, right sides together. **Note**: *Strip will be larger than center piece.* Stitch; finger-press open. Trim ends of strip as shown in Figure 2.

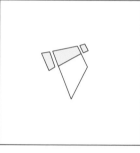

Figure 2

5. Continue stitching strips around the shape until the entire block is covered as shown in Figure 3; press.

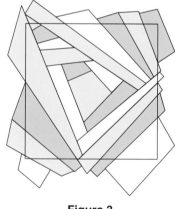

Figure 3

6. Work embroidery stitches over some seams by hand or machine using gold metallic thread in the top of the machine and off-white all-purpose thread in the bobbin. Press block; trim edges of strips even with edges of interfacing base. Repeat for 20 blocks.

7. Arrange blocks in four rows of five blocks each. Join blocks to make rows; join two rows to make one panel. Repeat to make two panels as shown in Figure 4.

Figure 4

8. Cut two 2" by fabric width strips binding fabric. Stitch one strip along one long edge of each panel to make a border. Press the raw edge of the border strip ½" to the wrong side.

9. Cut ribbing from hem and sleeves of sweatshirt.

10. Mark center-front line of sweatshirt with chalk pencil. Place one panel on each side of center front. Mark neckline and shoulder line on each panel with chalk pencil. Mark ¼"–½" larger (for seam allowance). Cut along outer line.

Optional Pockets

1. Place tracing paper over pocket pattern on page 13. Trace and cut out. Cut four pocket pieces from binding fabric, reversing two.

2. Place two pocket pieces right sides together. Stitch around outer edge with a ½" seam allowance, leaving end open as indicated on pattern. Repeat with remaining two pocket pieces. Press ¼" seam allowance to wrong side along one open end.

3. Place panels right side up on work surface. Open pressed edge of border strip. Pin one pocket on outer edge of each panel, 4"–6" from bottom with raw edges even and pressed seam allowance against panel. Stitch through panel and top layer only of pocket with a ¼" seam allowance. Fold to wrong side of panel; press.

Finishing

1. Press ¼"–½" toward wrong side along shoulder line and neckline of each panel.

2. Position panels along center-front line. Using clear nylon monofilament in the top of the machine and all-purpose thread in the bobbin, stitch panels in place along folded edge of border, hemline, neckline and shoulder line with blanket stitch, blind-hem stitch or narrow zigzag, leaving pocket area open. Baste ⅛" away from center-front line on each panel.

3. Press sweatshirt; cut along center-front line with sharp scissors.

4. Measure center front of sweatshirt from top to bottom. Cut two 4"-wide strips binding fabric this length plus ½" for plackets. Cut two 3"-wide strips fusible interfacing this same length. Center interfacing on wrong side of each strip; fuse in place, following manufacturer's directions.

5. Fold each strip in half along length with wrong sides together; press. Open fold; position one strip along the center-front line of each panel, right sides together. Stitch in place with a ½" seam allowance; press the seam allowances and placket toward the center line.

6. Fold the placket strip toward the wrong side; turn under ½" along remaining long raw edge. Stitch in place by hand or machine. Repeat on remaining center front. **Note:** *The project was topstitched through both placket layers using off-white thread. To stitch this way, it is best to baste the layers together to assure stitching is straight on both sides.*

7. Evenly space buttonholes in right front placket (as you are wearing it) to fit chosen buttons.

8. Stitch buttons on left front placket to match buttonholes.

9. Prepare 2 yards bias binding from binding fabric referring to General Instructions.

10. Cut ribbing off sleeve edges. Bind hemline and sleeve edges with prepared bias binding to finish as in General Instructions. ■

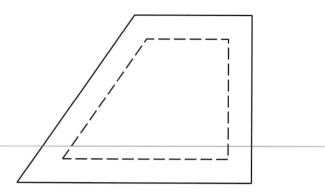
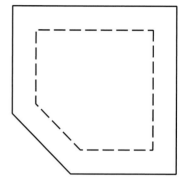
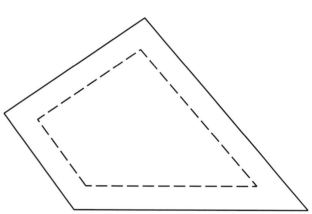

Center Templates

Heavenly Hash
Placement Diagram

Christmas Rose

BY BETH WHEELER

A bouquet of roses reflected by a frosty window inspired this intriguing pieced design.

FABRIC

- ⅜ yard rose stripe
- ⅜ yard medium rose print
- ⅜ yard each 2 rose-and-green prints
- ⅜ yard each 2 ivory prints
- ¾ yard dark rose print

TOOLS & SUPPLIES

- Light green sweatshirt with set-in sleeves
- Neutral color all-purpose thread
- Clear nylon monofilament
- Chalk pencil or fade-out pen
- Basic sewing tools and supplies, tracing paper, rotary cutter, mat and ruler

INSTRUCTIONS

1. Make a paper pattern for pocket piece (page 13) using tracing paper. Cut four pockets (two reversed) from the dark rose print. Cut two strips 1½" by fabric width from same fabric for edge strips and pocket binding.

2. Cut eight 1½"-wide strips at least 28" long from each fabric. Stitch strips together along length, stepping strips up ½" each time and alternating colors to create a pieced section with four pattern repeats as shown in Figure 1. Press seam allowances in one direction; repeat for a second pieced section with strips stepping down ½", again referring to Figure 1.

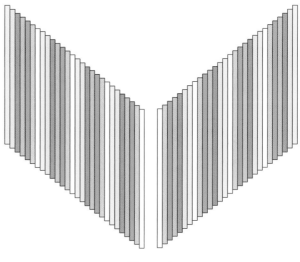

Figure 1

3. Cut seven 2" segments from each pieced section at a 60-degree angle as shown in Figure 2. Set aside one strip from each section to be used later for sleeves.

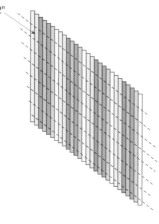

2"

Figure 2

4. Lay out 2" strip segments, alternating placement as shown in Figure 3. Stitch together along long edges with ¼" seam allowance. *Note: Pieced panel should be long enough to cover from shoulder line to top of hem ribbing, plus ¼" seam allowance.* Press seam allowances all in one direction.

Figure 3

5. Stitch a 1½"-wide dark rose print strip cut in step 1 to each long edge of pieced panel. Trim strip even with panel on both ends; press seams toward strips.

6. Cut ribbing from sweatshirt bottom. Cut sweatshirt to desired length. Fold sweatshirt in half referring to Figure 4. Mark center front with chalk pencil or fade-out pen.

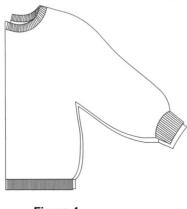

Figure 4

7. Place center of pieced panel along center-front line, with top edge ¼" above shoulder seam. Mark neckline and shoulder line on each side with chalk pencil or fade-out pen. Mark ¼" away from first line (for seam allowance); cut along outer line.

8. Place two pocket pieces together, right sides facing. Stitch around outer edge with a ½" seam allowance, leaving end open as indicated on pattern. Repeat with remaining two pocket pieces. Press ¼" seam allowance to wrong side along one side of each open end.

9. Place pieced panel right side up on work surface. Pin one pocket on outer edge of each panel 4"–6" from bottom, with raw edges even, and pressed seam allowance against panel. Stitch through panel and top layer only of pocket with a ¼" seam allowance referring to Figure 5. Fold pocket to wrong side of panel; press. Repeat for second pocket on other side.

Figure 5

10. Press ¼" toward wrong side along outer edge, bottom, shoulder and neckline of pieced panel. Position center of pieced panel along center-front line of sweatshirt; pin in place.

11. Stitch in place along all folded edges with a narrow zigzag or blind-hem stitch using monofilament in the top of the machine and all-purpose thread in the bobbin, leaving pocket area open.

12. Measure distance around armhole; use strips set aside in step 3 and cut to correct length; press ¼" under all around.

13. Pin a strip in place along each shoulder seam, allowing ½" between short ends at underarm to allow for stretch.

14. Stitch along folded edges with a narrow zigzag or blind-hem stitch using monofilament in the top of the machine and all-purpose thread in the bobbin.

15. Stitch ribbing back on sweatshirt along hemline or bind edge with self-made bias binding referring to General Instructions. ■

Christmas Rose
Placement Diagram

Trusty Rusty Bomber

BY BETH WHEELER

Here's a twist on the ever-popular bomber jacket, in autumn-inspired shades of rust and gold.

FABRIC
- 1 yard black-and-gold plaid for piecing, borders and binding
- ¼ yard each 6 or 7 gold-and-black print fabrics, including florals, plaids and checks

TOOLS & SUPPLIES
- Black sweatshirt with set-in sleeves
- Black all-purpose thread
- Clear nylon monofilament
- Black jacket zipper to fit front (do not purchase until after jacket is cut to length)
- Basic sewing tools and supplies

INSTRUCTIONS
1. Cut two strips 1¼", 1½", 1¾" or 2" from each fabric, varying width of same-fabric strips.

2. Stitch together in a section at least 15" wide. Press all seam allowances in one direction.

3. Cut four 4" segments from pieced section; stitch together along short ends to create one long panel referring to Figure 1. Panel should be as long as the circumference of sweatshirt below sleeves. Cut four 2" by fabric width strips from border fabric. Stitch two strips together on short ends to make one long strip; repeat to make two long border strips. Press seam allowances open.

Figure 1

4. Stitch one long edge of each border strip along each long edge of pieced panel, right sides together, as shown in Figure 2.

Figure 2

Finishing
1. Press seam allowance toward border. Press under ½" along one long edge of one border strip.

2. Cut hem ribbing off sweatshirt along waistline. Mark center-front line with chalk pencil (see General Instructions). Pin unpressed edge of wrong side of pieced panel to the right side of sweatshirt raw edge at hemline, beginning and ending at marked center front.

3. Topstitch in place along top folded edge using clear nylon monofilament in the top of the machine and black all-purpose thread in the bobbin and using a narrow zigzag or blind-hem stitch. Stitch along the hemline through the sweatshirt and pieced panel with a straight stitch to hold in place.

4. Carefully trim ribbing from removed strip. Pin and stitch ribbing back to sweatshirt along hemline of pieced panel.

5. Cut sweatshirt apart along center-front line. Prepare 1½ yards 2"-wide bias binding (see General Instructions). Fold ½" to wrong side along one long edge. Bind both front edges.

6. Insert zipper following manufacturer's instructions.

7. Cut several 2" segments from pieced panel as shown in Figure 3; stitch together along short ends to create two strips long enough to fit around sleeve at shoulder seam from back to front. Press under ¼"–½" along all four edges of each strip.

Figure 3

8. Pin in place along sleeve seam, beginning and ending at top of pieced panel. Stitch in place as for patchwork panel in step 3.

9. Cut sleeve off at desired length. Carefully cut cuff ribbing off removed piece. Stitch ribbing back on at desired length. ■

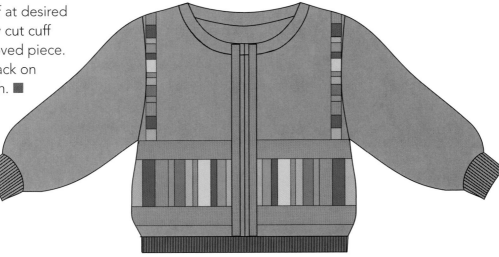

Trusty Rusty Bomber
Placement Diagram

Red Diamonds

BY BETH WHEELER

If you enjoy redwork, you'll love this design! Red and white patchwork accents the front panel and cuffs of this cozy cardigan.

FABRIC
- 1 yard red-and-white plaid for background and cuffs
- ½ yard red pin dot for borders, binding and piecing
- ⅛ yard each red-and-white stripe and floral print

TOOLS & SUPPLIES
- White sweatshirt with set-in sleeves
- Coordinating all-purpose thread
- Contrasting quilting thread or pearl cotton
- Clear nylon monofilament
- Chalk pencil or fade-out pen
- Basic sewing tools and supplies

Sweatshirt Front

1. Cut hem ribbing off sweatshirt bottom at desired finished length. **Note:** *Length of sweatshirt should be no less than 24" to make sure there is enough room for panel of three quilt blocks.* Cut neck ribbing off around neckline.

2. Mark center-front line of sweatshirt with chalk pencil or fade-out pen.

3. Cut two strips plaid 7½" by measurement of sweatshirt from highest shoulder point to hemline plus ½", measuring as shown in Figure 1. Cut two 2" strips by front measurement from red pin dot.

Figure 1

4. Place one long edge of pin dot along one long edge of plaid fabric, right sides together. Stitch; press seam allowance toward plaid fabric. Press ½" along remaining long raw edge of pin dot. Repeat with remaining piece of pin dot and plaid.

5. Position panels on sweatshirt with remaining long raw edge of plaid panel along center-front line as shown in Figure 2. Pin in place along center front and fold of pin-dot border.

Figure 2

6. Trim plaid panel even with sweatshirt along neck edge and shoulder seam or shoulder line, allowing ¼"–½" seam allowance along shoulder seam.

7. Turn seam allowance under along shoulder line; press. Stitch panels in place along border edge and across shoulder seam with narrow zigzag or blind-hem stitch using clear nylon monofilament in the top of the machine and thread to match sweatshirt in the bobbin. Baste ⅛" away from center-front line on each panel.

8. Cut seven 3½" x 3½" squares floral print, 28 pieces stripe fabric 1¼" x 3½" and 28 squares pin-dot fabric 1¼" x 1¼".

9. Sew a 1¼" x 3½" stripe strip to opposite sides of a floral print square. Sew a 1¼" x 1¼" pin-dot square to opposite ends of two 1¼" x 3½" stripe strips; sew to opposite sides of the pieced unit to complete one block as shown in Figure 3. Repeat for seven blocks; press. Set one block aside for sleeves.

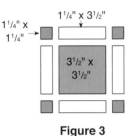

Figure 3

10. Position three squares on each panel along each side of center-front line as shown in Figure 4; pin in place.

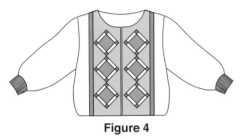

Figure 4

11. Work a narrow zigzag stitch around each block with clear nylon monofilament.

12. Work blanket stitch around each block by machine with contrasting quilting thread or by hand with pearl cotton as shown in Figure 5.

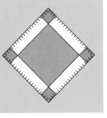

Figure 5

13. Cut sweatshirt open along marked center-front line. Prepare at least 4 yards bias binding from red pin dot referring to General Instructions. Bind center-front, hemline and neck edge with binding, again referring to the General Instructions.

Sleeves

1. Cut sleeve ribbing off each sleeve at desired length.

2. Cut four pieces 4" by the circumference of sleeve, plus 1", from plaid fabric.

3. Place two plaid pieces right sides together; stitch along one long edge with a ½" seam allowance. Press seam allowances open to complete one cuff; repeat for second cuff.

4. Cut remaining block in half on one diagonal as shown in Figure 6. Position one half-block section on one cuff as shown in Figure 7. Stitch in place using clear nylon monofilament in the top of the machine and all-purpose thread in the bobbin. Work blanket stitch around block as for front panel.

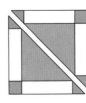

Figure 6   **Figure 7**

Continued on page 34

Tarantella Tracks

BY BETH WHEELER

Fusible bias tape forms the graceful curving design on this tarentella-inspired bolero.

PROJECT NOTE

To negotiate tight curves smoothly, use a narrow zigzag stitch and drop your sewing machine feed dogs for instant turning ability. Be careful when using this technique; it's easy to get ahead of yourself.

FABRIC

- Cranberry sweatshirt in desired size

TOOLS & SUPPLIES

- Black all-purpose thread
- 6 yards black ¼"-wide fusible bias tape
- 2 packages black extra-wide, double-fold bias tape
- 1 yard iron-on, peel-off stabilizer
- Iron wand or craft iron
- Dinner plate
- Basic sewing tools and supplies, paper and chalk pencil

INSTRUCTIONS

1. Cut neck, cuff and hem ribbing off sweatshirt.

2. Cut sweatshirt to desired length.

3. Find center front of sweatshirt referring to the General Instructions; draw a line using chalk pencil. Cut on drawn line. Use a dinner plate to round the bottom front center edges as shown in Figure 1.

Figure 1

4. Bind all raw edges using black extra-wide, double-fold bias tape.

5. Draw a looping pattern on a large piece of paper until you develop a pleasing pattern for front of sweatshirt as shown in Figure 2. Transfer the design to each side of the sweatshirt front with chalk pencil. Repeat for a design for the back.

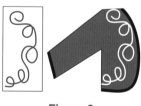

Figure 2

6. Turn under ⅛" on end of black ¼"-wide fusible bias tape. Beginning at the shoulder line, place bias tape along chalk line, working just a few inches at a time; secure in place with iron wand or craft iron. Repeat on all marked lines.

7. Bond iron-on, peel-off stabilizer to the wrong side of the sweatshirt behind bias tape following manufacturer's directions.

8. Stitch bias tape in place through sweatshirt and stabilizer using a narrow zigzag stitch. When stitching is complete, remove stabilizer.

9. Press sweatshirt thoroughly with steam iron for finished look. ■

Tarantella Tracks Front View
Placement Diagram

Tarantella Tracks Back View
Placement Diagram

Adobe Sunset

BY BETH WHEELER

Pieced Log Cabin blocks in sunset colors make a perfect border for a zip-front, bomber-style sweatshirt.

FABRIC
- Yellow, peach, pink, orange and red solid or print scraps
- ¼ yard red solid
- ½ yard orange mottled

TOOLS & SUPPLIES
- Yellow sweatshirt in desired size
- Yellow all-purpose thread
- Clear nylon monofilament
- Jacket zipper to fit sweatshirt front after cutting
- Basic sewing tools and supplies, chalk pencil, rotary cutter, mat and ruler

INSTRUCTIONS

1. Cut 10 squares 1½" x 1½" from different scraps for Log Cabin centers.

2. Cut a variety of 1¼"-wide strips from different scraps for Log Cabin strips.

3. To piece one block, sew a square to a 1¼"-wide strip as shown in Figure 1; press seam toward strip. Trim strip even with square. Sew this unit to the same 1¼"-wide strip as shown in Figure 2; press and trim as before. Continue until center square is surrounded by the same-fabric strips as shown in Figure 3.

4. Add a second 1¼"-wide fabric strip around all sides of the pieced unit to complete one Log Cabin block as shown in Figure 4; repeat for 10 blocks.

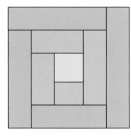

Figure 4

5. Cut four squares red solid 7" x 7"; cut each square in half on both diagonals to make A triangles. Cut two squares red solid 3¾" x 3¾"; cut each square on one diagonal to make B triangles.

6. Sew an A triangle to two opposite sides of six Log Cabin blocks as shown in Figure 5. Sew A to one side of the remaining two blocks as shown in Figure 6. Join the pieced units to make a strip as shown in Figure 7. Sew a B triangle to each angled end of the strip, again referring to Figure 7.

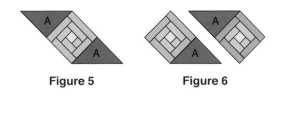

Figure 5   **Figure 6**

Figure 7

Figure 1

Figure 2

Figure 3

7. Cut and piece two 2" x 45¾" strips orange mottled. Sew a strip to opposite long sides of the pieced strip; press seams toward strips. Press under raw edge of one long edge of strip ⅜".

8. Find center-front line of sweatshirt referring to the General Instructions; mark with chalk pencil. Cut along marked line. Remove cuff from bottom of sleeves and ribbing from sweatshirt bottom. Cut sweatshirt to desired length. *Note: The sample was cut 1" below waistline to make bomber-style jacket.*

9. Fold top edge of neck ribbing under at center front and stitch in place as shown in Figure 8.

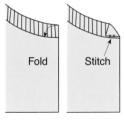

Figure 8

10. Find and mark center of pieced strip. Find and mark center of back bottom edge of sweatshirt. Match centers and pin the pieced strip to the bottom edge of the sweatshirt with raw edge of pieced strip even with raw edge of sweatshirt.

11. Sew pieced panel to sweatshirt along top folded edge of strip using a machine blind-hem stitch and clear nylon monofilament in the top of the machine and all-purpose thread in the bobbin. Machine-baste bottom edge of pieced panel to sweatshirt.

12. Sew removed sweatshirt bottom ribbing back on bottom of sweatshirt using a serger or narrow seam allowance and overcast zigzag stitch.

13. Prepare 2 yards 2"-wide orange mottled bias

binding referring to the General Instructions. Fold ½" to the wrong side along one long edge. Bind both center-front edges, finishing top and bottom of each front binding piece.

14. Insert zipper along center front referring to zipper manufacturer's instructions.

15. Finish sleeve bottoms using orange mottled bias binding referring to the General Instructions.

16. Cut a variety of 2"-wide strips of all fabrics. Join with right sides together along length to make a strip set as shown in Figure 9; press seams in one direction. Cut strip set into 1¼" segments.

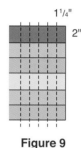

Figure 9

17. Measure around armhole; join 1¼" segments to create a strip to equal armhole measurement plus 1". Press each long edge under ¼".

18. Pin a pieced-and-pressed strip around each armhole seam on the sweatshirt, overlapping ends and turning under top end ¼"; stitch in place using a machine blind-hem stitch and clear nylon monofilament in the top of the machine and all-purpose thread in the bobbin; stitch across overlapped ends.

19. Sew remaining 1¼"-wide segments to the sides of the remaining two Log Cabin blocks in the same manner as in steps 3 and 4 to make larger blocks as shown in Figure 10. Turn under edges of each block ¼" and press.

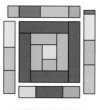

Figure 10

20. Try the sweatshirt on to determine elbow positions and mark with a pin. Center and pin a Log Cabin block to each sleeve, making sure each block is in the exact same location on sleeves. Stitch in place using a machine blind-hem stitch and clear nylon monofilament in the top of the machine and all-purpose thread in the bobbin.

21. Press sweatshirt thoroughly with steam iron for finished look. ◼

Adobe Sunset Front View
Placement Diagram

Adobe Sunset Back View
Placement Diagram

Adobe Color Blocks

BY BETH WHEELER

Bright blocks of color burst dramatically from a black background.

FABRIC

- ¼ yard each orange, turquoise, royal blue, navy, blue-violet, purple and black solids
- ½ yard red solid

TOOLS & SUPPLIES

- Black sweatshirt in desired size
- All-purpose thread to match sweatshirt
- Clear nylon monofilament
- 1½ yards drawstring cord
- 2 drawstring anchors
- 1¼" x 2" scrap fusible interfacing
- Basic sewing tools and supplies, chalk pencil, rotary cutter, mat and ruler

INSTRUCTIONS

1. Cut ribbing off hem of sweatshirt; cut sweatshirt to desired length. Even edges; press sweatshirt thoroughly with steam iron.

2. Cut varying fabric-width strips from the solid fabrics—1¼", 1½", 1¾", 1⅞", 2", 2¼", 2½", 2¾" and 3" were used in the sample.

3. Cut each strip in half to make two 20"–22"-long strips.

4. Stitch strips with right sides together along length in any color and width order to create a strip set at least 2" wider than the distance from the left underarm to the right underarm as shown in Figure 1; press seams in one direction. Repeat for two or three strip sets as needed.

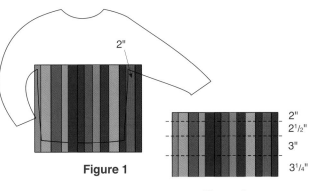

Figure 1

Figure 2

5. Cut each strip set into 2", 2½", 3" and 3¼" segments as shown in Figure 2.

6. Join the varying-width segments, offsetting colors, to create a panel at least 2" longer than the distance from the shoulder point at the neckline to the cut edge of the hemline as shown in Figure 3; press seams in one direction.

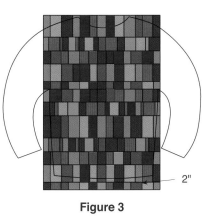

Figure 3

7. Mark a line down the center front of the sweatshirt using a chalk pencil. Fold the pieced panel and crease to find center. Center the pieced panel on the sweatshirt front, matching center lines, with top edge of panel ½" above shoulder seam; pin in place.

8. Mark the neckline at edge of ribbing, shoulder lines and side seams on the pieced panel using a chalk pencil. Mark ½" away from the first marked line for seam allowance. Remove panel from sweatshirt; cut along the outside marked line. *Note: Bottom edges should be longer than the sweatshirt at this time.*

9. Turn under seam allowance along the remaining marked line on the pieced panel; press to hold. Place pieced panel on sweatshirt front, again matching center lines. Align edges of panel with side seams, shoulder seam and neckline of sweatshirt; adjust folded seam allowance at this time, if necessary. Pin or baste in place.

10. Using clear nylon monofilament in the top of the machine and all-purpose thread in the bobbin, stitch pieced panel to sweatshirt at side and shoulder seams and along edge of neckline ribbing.

11. Press sweatshirt front; trim bottom edge of pieced panel even with sweatshirt bottom. Baste layers together.

12. Cut cuffs off sweatshirt sleeves.

13. Measure distance around sleeve edges and bottom edge of sweatshirt. Cut two 2½"-wide bias strips red solid by measured sleeve length plus 1" and one 2½"-wide by measured bottom length plus 1", joining strips as necessary as shown in Figure 4 to make the longer strip.

Figure 4
Join bias strips
as shown.

14. Sew across the ends of each short strip with right sides together using a ½" seam allowance to make a tube. Fold each tube in half with wrong sides together; press. Pin a folded tube to the bottom edge of each sleeve as shown in Figure 5; stitch. Finish seam with machine overcast stitch or serger. Fold bias strips down to make cuff and press. Topstitch ⅛" from seam on sweatshirt.

Figure 5

15. Fold the longer bias strip in half along length with wrong sides together; press. Unfold and mark the center. Fuse the scrap of fusible interfacing on the top half of the strip at the marked center. Center and stitch two buttonholes ½" apart on

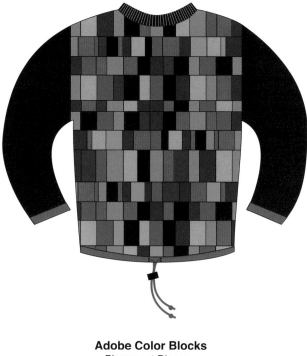

Adobe Color Blocks
Placement Diagram

the fused half of the strip as shown in Figure 6; cut openings.

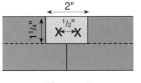

Figure 6

16. Stitch across short ends of the longer bias strip with right sides together using a ½" seam allowance to make a tube. Refold in half with wrong sides together and press; insert drawstring cord, pulling ends out through buttonholes. Center buttonhole section on front of sweatshirt; pin folded tube to hemline edge with right sides together and raw edges aligned and stitch to sweatshirt bottom as in step 14 to finish bottom edge. Topstitch ⅛" from seam on sweatshirt edge.

17. Thread drawstring cord ends through drawstring anchor; knot ends to finish. ■

Ladybug, Ladybug

BY BETH WHEELER

Busy little ladybugs scurry to and fro, leaving trails of hearts wherever they go.

PROJECT NOTES

Seam allowances are ¼" unless otherwise noted.

All binding can be completed from the same fabric, or using a different fabric for each edge.

FABRIC

- ¼ yard each red dot, red plaid and 2 navy prints
- 2" x 5" scrap black solid

TOOLS & SUPPLIES

- Blue sweatshirt with set-in sleeves
- Red and black rayon thread
- Blue topstitching thread or embroidery floss
- Clear nylon monofilament
- ⅛ yard fusible web
- ¼ yard iron-on, tear-away stabilizer
- 8 (1") red-heart appliqués
- ¾ yard ½"-wide elastic
- Chalk pencil or fade-out pen
- Basic sewing supplies and tools, rotary cutter, self-healing mat and ruler

INSTRUCTIONS

1. Cut three 1¼" by fabric width strips from each fabric.

2. Sew a red strip to a navy strip to a red strip using same red fabric twice; sew a navy strip to a red strip to a navy strip using same navy fabric twice. Press seam allowances toward darker strips.

Repeat with remaining red and navy strips to make a second set of strip sets.

3. Cut each strip set into 1¼" segments. Join same-fabric segments to make a Nine-Patch block as shown in Figure 1; repeat with second set of segments. Repeat for four Nine-Patch blocks from one set and five from the second set; press seams in one direction. Trim edges even, if necessary.

Figure 1

4. Cut nine squares fusible web 2¾" x 2¾". Bond one square to the wrong side of each block following manufacturer's directions; remove paper backing.

5. Cut hem ribbing off sweatshirt; cut sweatshirt to desired length.

6. Position alternating blocks along hemline around front edge of sweatshirt referring to the Placement Diagram and project photo for positioning; fuse in place.

7. Bond stabilizer to wrong side of sweatshirt, behind blocks.

8. Satin-stitch around each block with red rayon thread in the top of the machine and all-purpose thread in the bobbin; remove stabilizer.

9. Cut one strip from each fabric 2½" by fabric width. Sew strips together along length to make a pieced section; press seams in one direction. Cut strip into 1¾" segments.

10. Measure around armhole seam of sweatshirt. Join segments on short ends to make two strips this length. Press seam allowances all in the same direction. Press under ¼" on all sides.

11. Pin strips in place on sleeve along shoulder seam, leaving a ½" space between short ends at underarm. Stitch in place with a narrow zigzag or blind-hem stitch, using clear nylon monofilament in the top of the machine and all-purpose thread in the bobbin.

Finishing

1. Cut a 2½" x 7½" red dot scrap. Bond fusible web to wrong side of red dot and black solid following manufacturer's directions.

2. Prepare patterns for Ladybug Body and Head using patterns given.

3. Trace three bodies on paper side of red dot fabric. Trace three heads on paper side of black solid fabric. Cut out; remove paper backing.

4. Place bodies and heads on sweatshirt in desired positions, referring to the Placement Diagram and photo of project for suggested positioning; fuse in place.

5. Stitch detail lines on body and antennae using a narrow satin stitch and black rayon thread.

6. Satin-stitch around each head with black rayon thread. Satin-stitch around each body with red rayon thread.

7. Draw a meandering ladybug trail with chalk pencil, referring to Placement Diagram and photo for suggested placement.

8. Work a long running stitch along chalk-pencil line with heavy blue thread.

9. Hand-stitch heart appliqués in place along ladybug trail.

Binding

1. Make bias binding from leftover fabrics following directions on page 10.

2. Bind hem edge with bias binding.

3. Cut neck ribbing off sweatshirt; bind neck edge with bias binding.

4. Cut cuff ribbing off sleeves. Cut two 4"-wide pieces of another fabric long enough to fit around sleeve, plus 1".

5. Fold each piece in half along length with wrong sides together; press. Open fold on one piece and pin short ends together, right sides facing; stitch with a ½" seam allowance.

6. Fold one long edge under ½"; press. Stitch remaining long edge to sweatshirt sleeve, right sides together to make a casing.

7. Wrap folded edge to wrong side of sleeve, encasing raw edges. Stitch along fold, leaving an opening for inserting elastic. Cut a 12" piece of elastic. Insert elastic; close opening.

8. Repeat for second sleeve to finish. ■

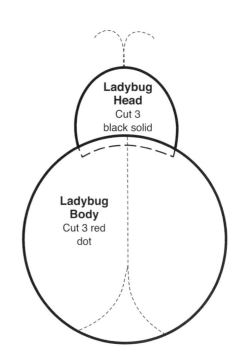

Ladybug
Head
Cut 3
black solid

Ladybug
Body
Cut 3 red
dot

Ladybug, Ladybug
Placement Diagram

Red Diamonds

Continued from page 23

5. Fold cuff section right sides together. Stitch across short ends with a ½" seam allowance as shown in Figure 8; press seam allowance open. Fold cuff with lining toward inside and block toward outside; press.

Figure 8

6. Pin cuff along outside edge of sleeve, with lining facing right side of sleeve. Stitch cuff to sleeve.

7. Tack cuff in place. Bind edge with bias binding made in step 13 for front. Repeat for remaining cuff. ■

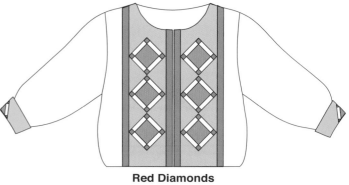

Red Diamonds
Placement Diagram

Lollipop Roses

BY BETH WHEELER

Appliquéd roses and a strip-pieced, scalloped hem add an elegant air to your wardrobe.

PROJECT NOTES

Enlarge or reduce scallop along dotted line to adjust to your sweatshirt.

Choose a sweatshirt one size larger than you usually wear. There is very little stretch at the hemline of this shirt.

FABRIC

- ¼ yard each of 3 pink prints
- ¼ yard each of 3 green prints

TOOLS & SUPPLIES

- White sweatshirt with set-in sleeves
- Pink and green all-purpose thread
- Pink and green rayon thread
- Green topstitching thread
- ½ yard fusible web
- 1 yard iron-on, tear-away stabilizer
- Chalk pencil or fade-out pen
- Basic sewing tools and supplies, rotary cutter, mat and ruler

INSTRUCTIONS

1. Cut two narrow strips (1¼", 1½" or 1¾") of each fabric across the width of the fabric. Cut each strip in half crosswise for two 22" strips for each width.

2. Stitch strips together along long edges, alternating colors and widths as shown in Figure 1. Press seam allowances in one direction.

3. Cut three 4"-wide segments, again referring to Figure 1; stitch together along short ends to create one strip. Cut into four sections to fit one

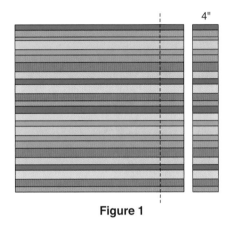

Figure 1

across the sweatshirt front, one across the back and two to fit around the sleeves.

4. Cut ribbing off sweatshirt at hemline; cut sleeves to desired length.

5. Bond stabilizer to wrong side of sweatshirt at hemline and sleeves following manufacturer's directions.

6. Press under ½" along short ends of each strip created in step 3. Position one long strip for sweatshirt front with wrong side of pieced strip along right side of cut sweatshirt with bottom edges even; pin or baste strips in place.

7. Make a pattern for scallop shape using pattern given.

8. Fold sweatshirt in half; press center line. Place scallop pattern on sweatshirt referring to Figure 2. Trace with chalk pencil or fade-out pen as shown in Figure 3. Stitch along marked line with a straight stitch.

9. Work a satin stitch around edges of scallops with green rayon thread in the top of the machine and green all-purpose thread in the bobbin.

10. Cut around scallop at bottom through all layers; cut around scallop at top through pieced strip only; remove stabilizer. Repeat with strips for back and sleeves.

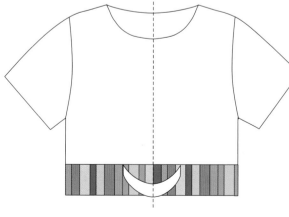

Figure 2

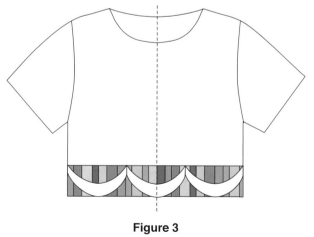

Figure 3

Flowers

1. Cut scraps from pink and green prints. Bond fusible web to the wrong side of scraps following manufacturer's directions.

2. Trace eight flowers on paper side of pink fabrics. Trace 13 leaves on paper side of green fabrics. Cut out on traced lines; remove paper backing.

3. Position flowers on sweatshirt referring to photo and Placement Diagram. Tuck leaves under edge of flowers; fuse in place. Bond stabilizer to wrong side of sweatshirt behind roses and leaves.

4. Buttonhole-stitch around each leaf using green topstitching thread in the top of the machine and

green all-purpose thread in the bobbin. Satin-stitch around spiral and outside edges of each flower using pink rayon thread; remove stabilizer.

5. Cut off neck ribbing. Bond stabilizer around neckline. Buttonhole-stitch around neckline using green topstitching thread; remove stabilizer. ▪

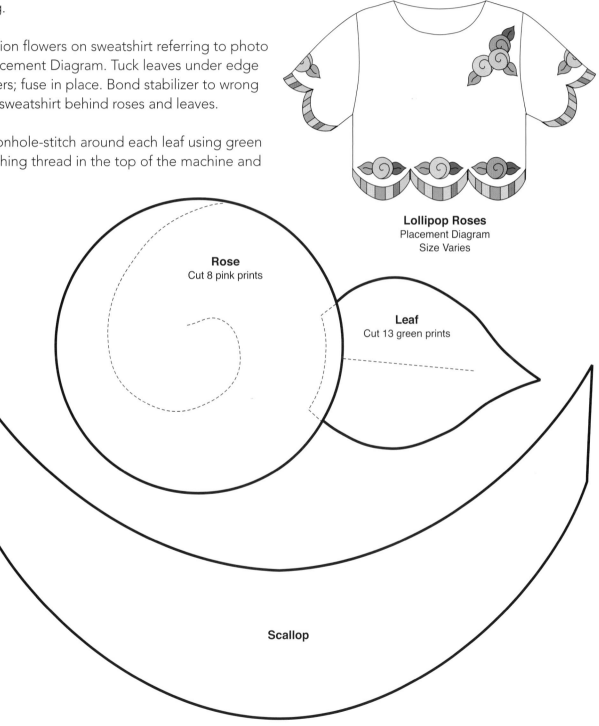

Lollipop Roses
Placement Diagram
Size Varies

Rose
Cut 8 pink prints

Leaf
Cut 13 green prints

Scallop

Southwest Diamond Vest

BY BETH WHEELER

The muted pastels of the desert southwest combine with folded fabric squares to accent this fleecy vest.

FABRIC

- ½ yard total assorted teal and turquoise prints, mottleds and solids for bias strips and binding strips
- 4 squares turquoise print 6" x 6" for A
- 4 squares teal print 6" x 6" for B
- ½ yard terra cotta solid

TOOLS & SUPPLIES

- Pale pink sweatshirt with set-in sleeves in desired size
- All-purpose thread to match fabrics
- Clear nylon monofilament
- 2 (1") abalone buttons
- Basic sewing tools and supplies, chalk pencil, rotary cutter, mat and ruler

INSTRUCTIONS

1. Cut sleeves off of sweatshirt along seam; remove ribbing from neckline and hemline.

2. Turn sweatshirt inside out; the fuzzy, fleece side will be the right side of the project.

3. Find and mark the center front of the sweatshirt referring to the General Instructions; cut along marked line.

4. Measure armhole opening and add ½";
prepare two 2½"-wide bias strips by this length.
Press under ½" on one long edge of each strip.
Sew each strip together on short ends to make a

tube. Pin remaining raw edge of each tube to the right side of armhole openings; stitch.

5. Press the bias strip to the inside of vest, enclosing raw edge of armhole openings; hand- or machine-stitch in place on inside of vest.

6. Place two 6" x 6" turquoise print A squares right sides together; stitch all around using a ¼" seam allowance. Trim corners; cut a slit in the center of one square, being careful not to cut through to second square. Turn right side out through cut slit; press to make square. Repeat for second set of squares.

7. Fold the squares with corners to the center as shown in Figure 1; tack corners in place in the centers.

Figure 1   **Figure 2**

8. Cut each B square in half on one diagonal to make eight B triangles.

9. Cut two squares terra cotta solid 8½" x 8½" for C. Sew a B triangle to each side of the C squares as shown in Figure 2; press seams toward B. Trim the B-C units to 11" x 11".

10. Cut two binding strips each 1" x 11" and 1" x 12". Sew the shorter strips to two opposite sides and longer strips to the top and bottom of each B-C unit as shown in Figure 3; press seams toward strips. Press under two adjacent sides of each unit ¼" as shown in Figure 4.

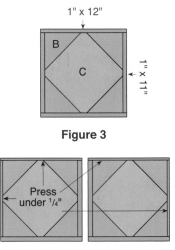

Figure 3

Figure 4

11. Center a folded A square on each B-C unit referring to the Placement Diagram for positioning; hand-stitch in place at each corner of A. Sew a button in the center of each A unit.

12. Prepare pattern for pocket piece (page 13); cut as directed on piece. Place one pocket and one reversed pocket piece right sides together; stitch around curved edges as shown in Figure 5 using a ½" seam allowance. Press a ¼" seam allowance under on each remaining straight edge. Repeat for second pocket set.

Figure 5

13. Place pieced panels right side up on work surface; open one folded edge as shown in Figure 6. Pin one pocket on outer edge of each panel 4"–6" from bottom, with raw edges even and pressed seam allowance of pocket toward panel as shown in Figure 7 on page 40.

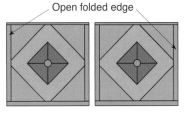

Open folded edge

Figure 6

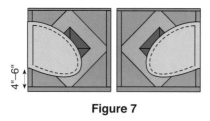

Figure 7

through the pocket back to attach to sweatshirt as shown in Figure 10. Continue stitching from opening to bottom edge through all layers.

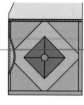

Figure 10

14. Stitch through the panel and top layer only of the pocket using a ¼" seam allowance. Fold to wrong side of panel; press.

15. Position one panel/pocket unit on each front with pressed seam allowance at the top, folded seam allowance with pocket in it to the side, and raw edges of unit even with raw cut edges of sweatshirt as shown in Figure 8.

17. Machine-baste panel to bottom and center-front edges.

18. Repeat steps 4 and 5 to complete bias binding for center front, neckline and bottom edges. Bind bottom edge and then neckline edge; bind center-front edge last to finish. ■

Figure 8

16. Stitch across top folded edge of panel unit using clear nylon monofilament in the top of the machine and all-purpose thread in the bobbin. Pivot at the unit corner; stitch down to the pocket opening through all layers to secure as shown in Figure 9. Hold the pocket front open and stitch

Figure 9

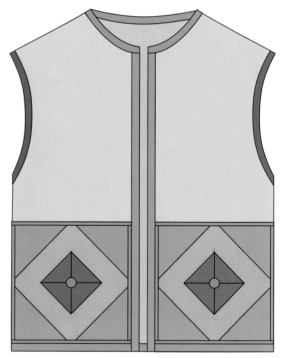

Southwest Diamond Vest
Placement Diagram

I'm a Little Angel

BY KATE LAUCOMER

A guardian angel watches over your favorite child from the front of a cozy sweatshirt.

FABRIC
- Scraps green and cream prints

TOOLS & SUPPLIES
- 1 child-size red sweatshirt
- ½ yard green print
- Red all-purpose thread
- Variegated rayon thread
- ⅛ yard fusible web
- ¼ yard tear-off fabric stabilizer
- 7 (¾") white star buttons
- 2 (½") white star buttons
- Basic sewing tools and supplies

INSTRUCTIONS

1. Carefully remove all ribbing at neck, cuffs and waist of sweatshirt. **Note:** *It is easier to undo the stitching than to cut off these areas.* Be careful not to stretch the neckline.

2. Prepare 2 yards 3"-wide bias binding from green print referring to the General Instructions.

3. Measure around the neckline of the sweatshirt; add ½". Cut a piece of bias binding this length; join on short ends to make a tube.

4. Press tube in half with wrong sides together as shown in Figure 1.

Figure 1

5. Evenly space and pin bias tube to right side of neck edge; sew all around using a ½" seam allowance. **Note:** *Before the next step, try the sweatshirt on the child, if possible, to be sure the neck opening is large enough.*

6. Trim the green fabric in the seam allowance to ¼"; turn binding to the wrong side. Hand-stitch in place.

7. Trim length of sweatshirt at this time to make a shorter shirt, if desired.

8. Measure around sweatshirt bottom edge; add ½" to this measurement. Prepare a bias tube as in steps 3 and 4.

9. Pin the tube right sides together with the bottom edge of the sweatshirt; sew using a ½" seam allowance.

10. Turn to wrong side; hand-stitch in place.

11. Trim sleeves to desired length. Measure cuff edge and add ½" to the measurement.

12. Cut two strips green print 3½" by the measurement in step 11 for cuffs.

13. Sew the short ends of one strip with right sides together to make a tube. Press tube in half with wrong sides together; repeat for second cuff piece.

14. Pin tube to the wrong side of the sweatshirt; sew. Turn over seam to the right side to create the cuff; press in place.

15. Sew a ½" white star button on upper edge of each cuff to hold in place.

16. Trace angel parts onto the paper side of the fusible web. Cut out shapes, leaving a margin around each one. **Note:** *To avoid the darker sweatshirt showing through lighter fabrics, you may want to fuse two layers of lighter fabrics together before tracing shapes. Treat like one layer of fabric when cutting.*

17. Fuse shapes to the wrong side of fabrics as directed on pattern. Cut out shapes on traced lines; remove paper backing.

18. Position the angel shapes on the center front of the sweatshirt referring to the Placement Diagram for positioning suggestions. Fuse shapes in place in numerical order.

19. Pin tear-off fabric stabilizer behind fused shapes. Using variegated rayon thread in the top of the machine and all-purpose thread in the bobbin, machine satin-stitch around each shape. When stitching is complete, tear off stabilizer.

20. Arrange ¾" white star buttons around appliquéd shape. Hand-stitch in place to finish. ■

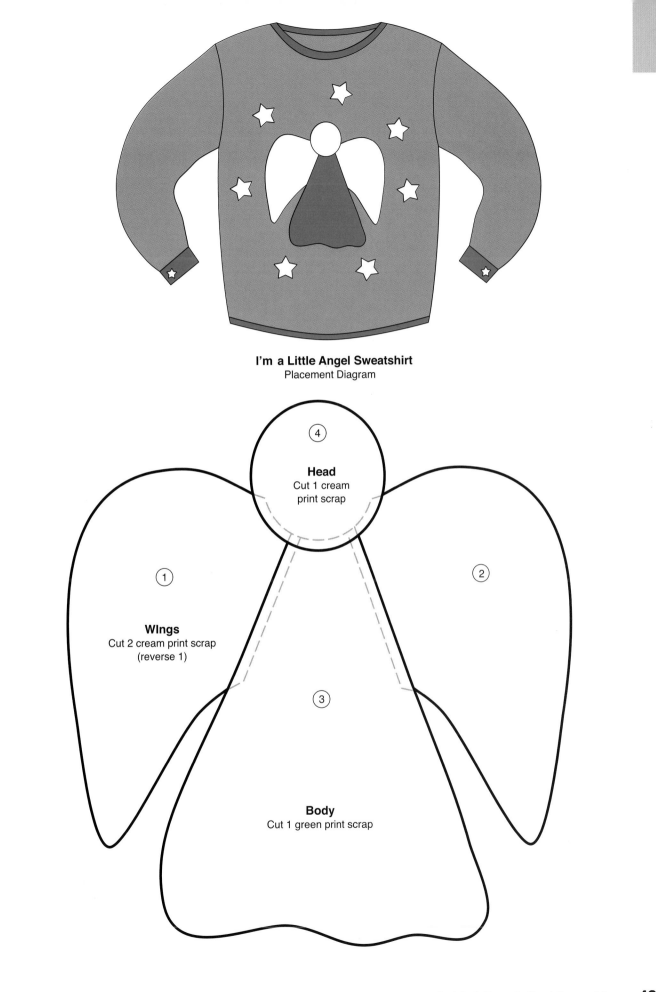

I'm a Little Angel Sweatshirt
Placement Diagram

④

Head
Cut 1 cream
print scrap

① ②

Wings
Cut 2 cream print scrap
(reverse 1)

③

Body
Cut 1 green print scrap

Let's Fly A Kite

BY VICKI BLIZZARD

Four-patch kites float on rick-rack strings among fluffy clouds on the front of this child-size sweatshirt.

FABRIC

- Scraps of white, blue, red, yellow and green prints

TOOLS & SUPPLIES

- Child's sweatshirt in desired size
- White and neutral color all-purpose thread
- 1 package white baby rickrack
- Fray preventive
- Basic sewing tools and supplies

INSTRUCTIONS

1. Prepare templates using pattern pieces given. Cut as directed on each piece.

2. Join two each red and blue print A squares to make a Four-Patch block as shown in Figure 1. Repeat with green and yellow prints to make a second block.

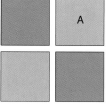

Figure 1

3. Turn under edges of cloud pieces. Hand-appliqué in place on sweatshirt referring to the photo and Placement Diagram for positioning to finish.

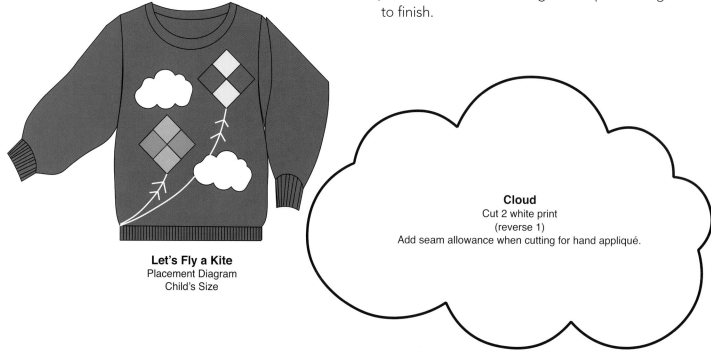

Let's Fly a Kite
Placement Diagram
Child's Size

Cloud
Cut 2 white print
(reverse 1)
Add seam allowance when cutting for hand appliqué.

4. Cut two lengths rickrack for kite tails referring to the Placement Diagram for positioning and measuring the sweatshirt for desired length. ***Note:*** *Sample lengths are 7" and 13" long.* Using white thread, hand- or machine-stitch rickrack in place.

5. Turn under edges of each Four-Patch unit ¼" all around; pin corner of block to top of stitched rickrack. Hand-appliqué blocks in place with neutral color thread.

6. Cut four pieces rickrack each 3" long. Tie a knot in the center of each piece. Trim ends to approximately 1"; apply fray preventive to each end.

7. Hand-stitch a knotted piece of rickrack to previously stitched rickrack at the knot to make kite tails; leave ends free. ■

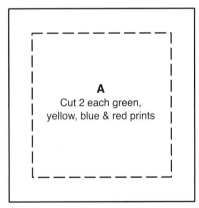

A
Cut 2 each green,
yellow, blue & red prints

Little Sheriff Vest

BY JANICE LOEWENTHAL

Your little cowboy can tame the Wild West with his stick horse and sheriff's badge.

FABRIC
- Brown child-size sweatshirt with set-in sleeves
- Scraps rust, stripe, gold, tan and brown

TOOLS & SUPPLIES
- Thread to match appliqué fabrics
- ⅓ yard fusible web
- ¼ yard tear-off fabric stabilizer
- 1 package rust single-fold bias tape
- 1 yard purchased 2¼"-wide rust fringe
- Black and white permanent fabric pens
- Basic sewing tools and supplies, water-erasable marker and straightedge

INSTRUCTIONS
1. Use a water-erasable marker and straightedge to draw a line down the center front of the sweatshirt; cut open along line.

2. Carefully remove the bottom ribbing and sleeves from the sweatshirt.

3. Unfold one edge of the rust single-fold bias tape; align the outer edge of the tape with the bottom edge of the sweatshirt with right sides together; stitch along the pressed line of the bias tape. Turn to wrong side of sweatshirt; press. Repeat on front and sleeve openings. Hand-stitch binding in place.

4. Prepare patterns for appliqué pieces using full-size patterns given. Trace shapes on paper side of fusible web; cut out shapes leaving a margin around traced line.

5. Fuse paper shapes onto wrong side of fabric scraps as directed on patterns for color. Cut out shapes on traced lines; remove paper backing.

6. Arrange hat motif on one side and pony motif on other side of vest front, layering pieces as necessary and referring to the Placement Diagram and photo of project for positioning of pieces. Fuse pieces in place.

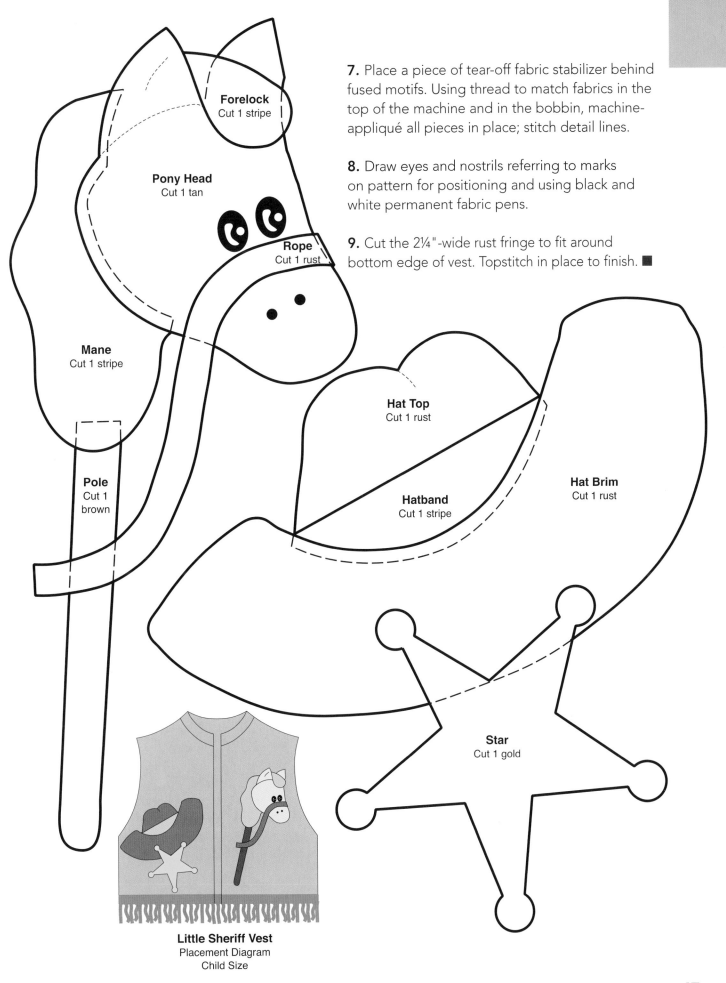

Forelock
Cut 1 stripe

Pony Head
Cut 1 tan

Rope
Cut 1 rust

Mane
Cut 1 stripe

Pole
Cut 1 brown

Hat Top
Cut 1 rust

Hatband
Cut 1 stripe

Hat Brim
Cut 1 rust

Star
Cut 1 gold

7. Place a piece of tear-off fabric stabilizer behind fused motifs. Using thread to match fabrics in the top of the machine and in the bobbin, machine-appliqué all pieces in place; stitch detail lines.

8. Draw eyes and nostrils referring to marks on pattern for positioning and using black and white permanent fabric pens.

9. Cut the 2¼"-wide rust fringe to fit around bottom edge of vest. Topstitch in place to finish. ■

Little Sheriff Vest
Placement Diagram
Child Size

Metric Conversion Charts

Metric Conversions

U.S. Measurements		Multiplied by	Metric Measurement
yards	x	.9144	= meters (m)
yards	x	91.44	= centimeters (cm)
inches	x	2.54	= centimeters (cm)
inches	x	25.40	= millimeters (mm)
inches	x	.0254	= meters (m)

Metric Measurements		Multiplied by	U.S. Measurements
centimeters	x	.3937	= inches
meters	x	1.0936	= yards

Standard Equivalents

U.S. Measurement		Metric Measurement		
1/8 inch	=	3.20 mm	=	0.32 cm
1/4 inch	=	6.35 mm	=	0.635 cm
3/8 inch	=	9.50 mm	=	0.95 cm
1/2 inch	=	12.70 mm	=	1.27 cm
5/8 inch	=	15.90 mm	=	1.59 cm
3/4 inch	=	19.10 mm	=	1.91 cm
7/8 inch	=	22.20 mm	=	2.22 cm
1 inch	=	25.40 mm	=	2.54 cm
1/8 yard	=	11.43 cm	=	0.11 m
1/4 yard	=	22.86 cm	=	0.23 m
3/8 yard	=	34.29 cm	=	0.34 m
1/2 yard	=	45.72 cm	=	0.46 m
5/8 yard	=	57.15 cm	=	0.57 m
3/4 yard	=	68.58 cm	=	0.69 m
7/8 yard	=	80.00 cm	=	0.80 m
1 yard	=	91.44 cm	=	0.91 m

Embroidery Stitch Guide

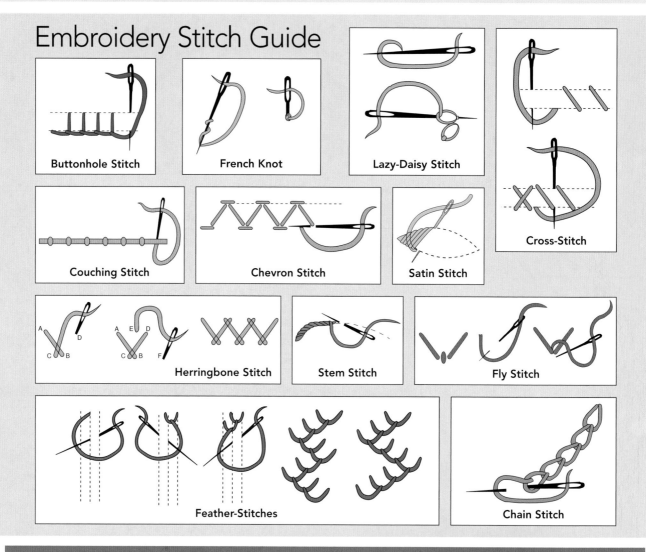

Buttonhole Stitch

French Knot

Lazy-Daisy Stitch

Cross-Stitch

Couching Stitch

Chevron Stitch

Satin Stitch

Herringbone Stitch

Stem Stitch

Fly Stitch

Feather-Stitches

Chain Stitch

E-mail: Customer_Service@whitebirches.com

HOUSE of WHITE BIRCHES PUBLISHERS SINCE 1947

Quick & Easy Quilted Sweatshirts is published by House of White Birches, 306 East Parr Road, Berne, IN 46711, telephone (260) 589-4000. Printed in USA. Copyright © 2006 House of White Birches.

RETAIL STORES: If you would like to carry this pattern book or any other House of White Birches publications, call the Wholesale Department at Annie's Attic to set up a direct account: (903) 636-4303. Also, request a complete listing of publications available from House of White Birches.

ISBN: 1-59217-096-X
2 3 4 5 6 7 8 9

STAFF
Editors: Jeanne Stauffer, Sandra L. Hatch
Associate Editor: Dianne Schmidt
Technical Artist: Connie Rand
Copy Supervisor: Michelle Beck
Copy Editors: Nicki Lehman, Mary O'Donnell, Judy Weatherford

Graphic Arts Supervisor: Ronda Bechinski
Graphic Artists: Debby Keel, Edith Teegarden
Art Director: Brad Snow
Assistant Art Director: Nick Pierce

Every effort has been made to ensure that the instructions in this pattern book are complete and accurate. We cannot, however, take responsibility for human error, typographical mistakes or variations in individual work.